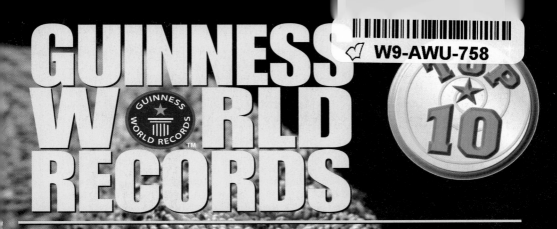

GUINNESS WORLD RECORDS

TOP 10

Incredible Reptile Records

Compiled by Celeste Lee and Ryan Herndon

For Guinness World Records:
Laura Barrett Plunkett, Craig Glenday, Stuart Claxton,
Michael Whitty, and Laura Jackson

SCHOLASTIC INC.
New York   Toronto   London   Auckland   Sydney
Mexico City   New Delhi   Hong Kong   Buenos Aires

The publisher would like to thank the following for
their kind permission to use their photographs in this book:

Cover, title page Adult Komodo Dragon © Martin Harvey/CORBIS; 1 Juvenile Komodo Dragon © Michael Pitts/Nature
Picture Library; 2 Amphibian Atop Reptile © Art Wolfe/Stone/Getty Images; 4 Allosaurus Illustration © Joe Tucciarone/
Photo Researchers, Inc.; 5 Tuatara © John Markham/Bruce Coleman USA; 6 (top) Indian Gharial © Anup Shah/Nature
Picture Library, (bottom) Dwarf Caiman © Claus Meyer/Minden Pictures; 7 Supercroc Model © Will Burgess/Reuters;
8 Steve Irwin © Justin Sullivan/Getty Images; 9 Harriet the Galapagos Tortoise © Cameron Laird/REX USA; 10 Speckled
Cape Tortoise © Suzanne L. and Joseph T. Collins/Photo Researchers, Inc.; 11 Aldabra and Speckled Padloper Tortoises
© Anthony Bannister/Photo Researchers, Inc.; 12 Galapagos Tortoise in Zoo © Chuck Kirman, Ventura County Star/AP
Wide World Photos; 13 Lonesome George © Morley Read/naturepl.com; 14 Pygmy Chameleon © Martin Harvey,
Gallo Images/CORBIS; 15 Slow Worm © Colin Seddon/Nature Picture Library; 16 (top) Beaver-Tailed Day Gecko
© David A. Northcott/CORBIS, (bottom) Chameleon © Stephen Dalton/Animals Animals - Earth Scenes; 17 Komodo
Dragon © Cyril Ruoso/JH Editorial/Minden Pictures; 18 Dwarf Gecko © S. Blair Hedges 2001; 19 Texas Horned Lizard
© Joe McDonald/CORBIS; 20 Spiny-Tailed Iguana © Patricio Robles Gil/Nature Picture Library; 21 Yellow Anaconda
© Tom Brakefield/Jupiter Images; 22 Anaconda Wrestling Caiman © Martin Wendler/NHPA; 23 Green Anaconda
© Heinz Plenge/Peter Arnold, Inc./Alamy; 24 Antiguan Racer © John Cancalosi/Peter Arnold, Inc.; 25 Black Mamba
© R. Andrew Odum/Peter Arnold, Inc.; 26 (top) Saw-Scaled Viper © Barry Mansell/Nature Picture Library, (bottom)
Infrared View © Joseph Paduano/Nonstock/Jupiter Images; 28 Blue Coral Snake © Frank Lane Picture Agency/CORBIS;
29 Antivenin © Cardoso/Oxford Scientific Films; 30 Parsons Chameleon © Ingo Arndt/Foto Natura/Minden Pictures.

Guinness World Records Limited has a very thorough accreditation system
for records verification. However, while every effort is made to ensure accuracy,
Guinness World Records Limited cannot be held responsible for any
errors contained in this work. Feedback from our readers on
any point of accuracy is always welcomed.

ISBN-13: 978-0-439-87417-5
ISBN-10: 0-439-87417-3

Designed by Michelle Martinez Design, Inc.
Photo Research by Els Rijper, Alan Gottlieb
Records from the Archives of Guinness World Records

12 11 10 9 8 7 6 5 4   8 9 10 11/0

Printed in the U.S.A.

First printing, January 2007

Visit Guinness World Records at www.guinnessworldrecords.com

Reptiles are experts at survival.
Many kinds of reptiles have roamed Earth
for more than 300 million years!

This *Guinness World Records*™ book zips through time
with 10 record-setting reptiles, from a prehistoric
crocodile to a modern-day dragon.

TIPPING THE SCALES

Animals change, or evolve, to stay alive because the world around them keeps changing. Millions of years ago, one animal evolved into many different types, or species. Today, there are mammals, fish, insects, birds, amphibians, and reptiles.

A reptile has a backbone, uses lungs to breathe air, and is cold-blooded. This means its body heat is the same as the outdoor temperature. Hard scales cover its skin. Baby reptiles hatch from eggs and look like adults, only smaller.

A dart frog is an *amphibian*.

A caiman is a *reptile*.

Reptiles have evolved into many shapes and sizes. Now, there are more than 8,000 different kinds of reptiles (see chart below). Some slither through grass, sand, or water. A few grow homes atop their backs. Others stomp across the ground. These are today's living relatives of the dinosaurs.

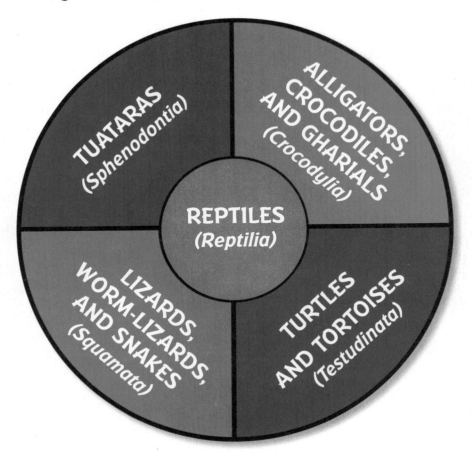

REPTILES
(Reptilia)

TUATARAS
(Sphenodontia)

ALLIGATORS, CROCODILES, AND GHARIALS
(Crocodylia)

LIZARDS, WORM-LIZARDS, AND SNAKES
(Squamata)

TURTLES AND TORTOISES
(Testudinata)

A **paleontologist** is a scientist who studies dinosaurs (below). The history of the word **dinosaur** can be traced back to mean "terrible lizard." These giant reptiles ruled our planet until 65 million years ago. Scientists believe a large asteroid hit Earth. Dust and smoke blocked the sunshine. The cold-blooded dinosaurs needed sunshine to keep their bodies warm. Many became **extinct**, or died. Others survived by evolving.

Dig up more dinosaur records in this book!

The closest link to the dinosaurs alive today is the **tuatara** (above). Their body shape has stayed the same for millions of years. Two types, *Sphenodon punctatus* and *Sphenodon guntheri*, creep around New Zealand. These reptiles survive lower temperatures better than others. They sleep in holes called **burrows**. A "third eye" hidden under its tough skin is used for telling time because the tuatara hunts only at night.

Alligators, crocodiles, and gharials are all **crocodilians**. These reptiles have strong jaws, thick skin, powerful tails, and hearts with four chambers. They live and hunt near water. Their eyes sit on top of their head, perfect for spying above the water. Look at their jaw shape to tell them apart. A gharial has a long, skinny snout (above). A crocodile's fourth tooth pokes through a hole in its upper jaw, while an alligator's broad snout hides its teeth. Caimans are small South American alligators (below).

Largest Crocodile Ever

Today, the **Largest Reptile** is the saltwater crocodile *(Crocodylus porosus)* of Asia and the Pacific, at a length of 23 feet. It eats smaller reptiles, fish, and mammals. Fossils found in the Sahara Desert show the **Largest Crocodile Ever** lived 110 million years ago and dined upon the dinosaurs! *Sarchosuchus imperator*, also nicknamed "Supercroc," was 40 feet long and weighed more than 17,600 pounds — that's longer than a bus and heavier than a truck. Its skull was 6 feet long and its giant jaws held 132 teeth (see model below).

Reptile Rescuer

Fearless "Crocodile Hunter" Steve Irwin (1962 - 2006) knew all about the reptiles in our world—and he loved them (above)! Steve learned to care for crocodiles and other reptiles from a young age at his parents' zoo. When he grew up, Steve worked closely with zoologists, scientists who study animals. He "hunted crocs" to study them and keep them safe from people known as poachers, who would hurt these animals to make money. Steve dedicated his life to teaching people about the need to protect these magnificent creatures and their natural habitat.

SHOCKING SHELLS

The great-grandparents of testudines (turtles and tortoises) made a big body change about 250 million years ago. They *grew* a home! This two-part shell is made of hard scales, or scutes — the same material as your fingernails. If danger is near, some testudines can pull their whole body inside their home.

The two shells are connected on the side.

The top shell is the carapace.

The bottom shell is the plastron.

9

Smallest Chelonian

Turtles mostly live in water, while tortoises live on land (below). Both groups share the scientific name of **chelonian**. There are 229 species of chelonian, living on every continent except Antarctica.

The speckled cape tortoise, or speckled padloper (*Homopus signatus*), is the **Smallest Chelonian**. This tiny tortoise has a shell length between only 2.3 to 3.7 inches. It lives in South Africa.

Archelon was a prehistoric turtle about the size of a car!

Size doesn't stop an animal from becoming extinct (above). Once there were 14 species of tortoises crawling in the Galapagos Islands in the Pacific Ocean, near Ecuador. Three are now extinct. How?

People are the biggest danger. Visiting sailors took the Galapagos tortoises because turtle soup and eggs made popular dishes. Commercial fishing nets accidentally trap turtles. Pollution makes survival tough, especially for sea turtles because they will eat plastic garbage tossed into the ocean.

Largest Tortoise

But there are also people who save reptiles, such as the Galapagos tortoises. Many of these giant creatures are born and raised in zoos or in a safe place known as a **sanctuary** (below). Later, the animals are returned to the Galapagos Islands and live in the wild.

The **Largest Tortoise** was a Galapagos tortoise *(Chelonoidis nigra)* named Goliath (not pictured). His shocking size was 4 feet 5 inches long, and 3 feet 4 inches wide. He weighed 920 pounds! From 1960 until 2002, Goliath lived at the Life Fellowship Bird Sanctuary in Seffner, Florida.

Rarest Reptile

People worried that another species of Galapagos tortoise had become extinct . . . until park rangers found the **Rarest Reptile** in 1971. This male Abingdon Island giant tortoise (*Geochelone elephantopus abingdoni*) is nicknamed "Lonesome George" because he is the last living example of his species. Scientists have not yet found any female tortoises, so George is lonely but still hopeful (see his chart below).

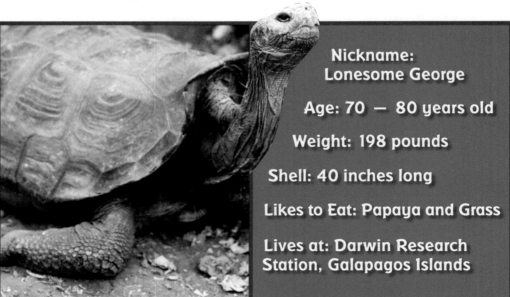

Nickname: Lonesome George

Age: 70 — 80 years old

Weight: 198 pounds

Shell: 40 inches long

Likes to Eat: Papaya and Grass

Lives at: Darwin Research Station, Galapagos Islands

A LIZARD'S LIFE

Snakes and lizards are squamates. Both use tongues to smell food and, every few months, peel off their skin like you pull off an old sock. Squamates can shift their mouths to swallow large meals. They've survived for millions of years because of their special skills and are the largest reptile group.

Fossils found in China and Mongolia of the Earliest Prehistoric Salamanders date 165 million years ago.

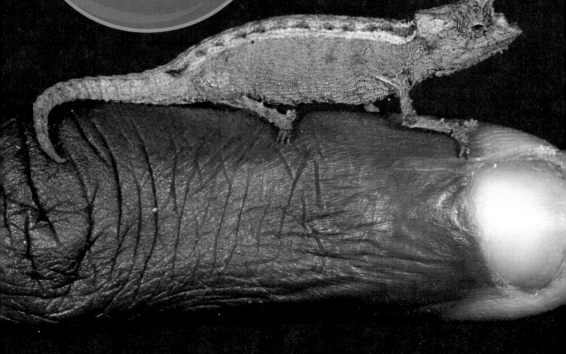

Some lizards called **worm-lizards** slither like snakes across the ground (above). The **Oldest Lizard** on record is a slow worm (*Anguis fragilis*). This lizard doesn't have legs! Slow worms eat spiders, insects, and snails. The record-holder lived in a Denmark zoo for 54 years (1892 – 1946).

This is one out of 4,500 lizard species — including iguanas, chameleons, geckos, Gila monsters, monitors, and skinks. Lizards come in both bright and dull-colored scales, huge and small sizes, but all have ears, eyelids, and bodies ending in a tail.

Most lizards have special skills. Many have tails that break off if grabbed, then regrow later. Iguanas boast a crest of spikes from neck to tail. Geckos can walk up walls because 2 million hairs make each foot sticky (right). Chameleons change their skin color to show their moods . . . then grab food with tongues about half as long as their bodies (below)!

Largest Lizard

Lizards evolve to live in the strangest places. The **Largest Lizard** is a modern-day dragon stomping across islands in Indonesia (below). In 1928, a Komodo dragon (*Varanus komodoensis*) measured 10 feet 2 inches long and weighed 365 pounds! These gigantic monitor lizards, or oras, eat deer, pig, and smaller dragons. One 100-pound Komodo ate a 90-pound pig in 20 minutes — that's like a 100-pound person eating 320 large hamburgers!

Smallest Lizard

The record for **Smallest Lizard** is divided between two dwarf geckos with names longer than their 0.6-inch long bodies. In 1964, *Sphaerodactylus parthenopion* was discovered on the Virgin Islands. In 2001, *Sphaerodactylus ariasae* was found on the island of Beata, West Indies. Out of a total 23,000 species of reptiles, birds, and mammals, these geckos are small enough to curl up on a dime (below)! Even if caught, these lizards can snap off their tail and scurry away. Don't worry, the tail grows back.

Strangest Defense Mechanism

The Texas horned lizard (*Phrynosoma cornutum*) is nicknamed "horny toad" — but it's not an amphibian (left)! This reptile is just 6 inches long, but it hides the **Strangest Defense Mechanism**. This fierce-looking lizard has horns on its head and pointy spines. If danger comes near, this reptile flattens its body against the ground. It lightens or darkens its skin color to match the ground, an example of **camouflage**. If the lizard still can't get away, then it squirts poisonous blood from holes near its eyes!

Triple Threat

These three reptiles can really protect themselves. The Longest Lizard is the Salvadori or Papuan monitor *(Varanus salvadorii)* of Papua New Guinea. It measured 15 feet 7 inches long with a powerful tail of 10 feet — watch out!

The Most Dangerous Lizard is the Gila monster *(Heloderma suspectum)* of Mexico and the southwestern United States. This colorful lizard's beaded scales are like the dinosaur's skin. Although less than 2 feet long, its bite is big trouble! Its tiny teeth break the victim's skin and poison seeps in.

The Fastest Lizard is *Ctenosaura*, a spiny-tailed iguana of Central America (left). Running only on its two hind legs, its speed has been clocked at 21.7 miles per hour — that's *speedier* than the Fastest Land Snake (see Record 9)!

SPECTACULAR SNAKES

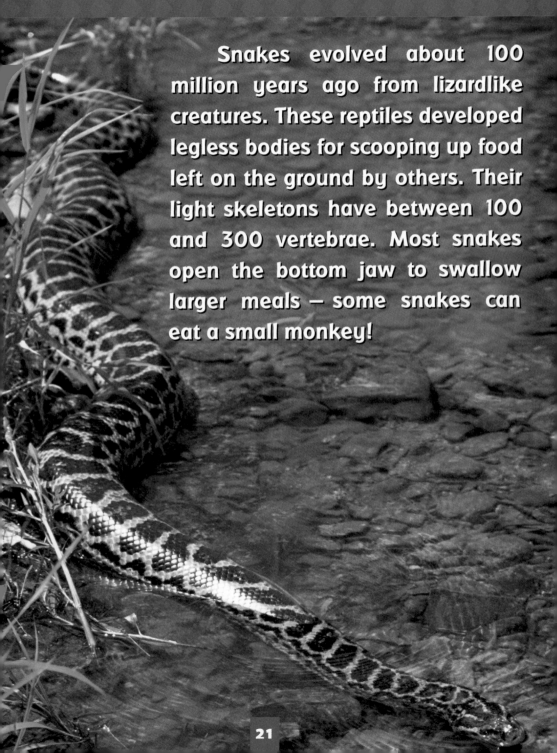

Snakes evolved about 100 million years ago from lizardlike creatures. These reptiles developed legless bodies for scooping up food left on the ground by others. Their light skeletons have between 100 and 300 vertebrae. Most snakes open the bottom jaw to swallow larger meals — some snakes can eat a small monkey!

About 20 percent of snakes strike and deliver **venom**, or poison, through their fangs. Other snakes, such as boas and pythons, attack by **constriction** (below). Their bodies wrap around the prey, and the muscles *squeeze* until the prey's heart stops.

Paleontologists found a 38-million-year-old Egyptian fossil of the Longest Prehistoric Snake. *Gigantophis garstini* was python-like at 36 feet long — the length of a school bus!

Anacondas are a species of boa constrictor. This snake's enormous size and weight help it swallow large animals and *really* tip the scales. The **Heaviest Snake** is the green anaconda of South America and Trinidad (below). A swimmer in Venezuela's swamps, this record-holding female was caught in 1960. She was 27 feet 9 inches long and 44 inches thick . . . and broke the scales at 500 pounds!

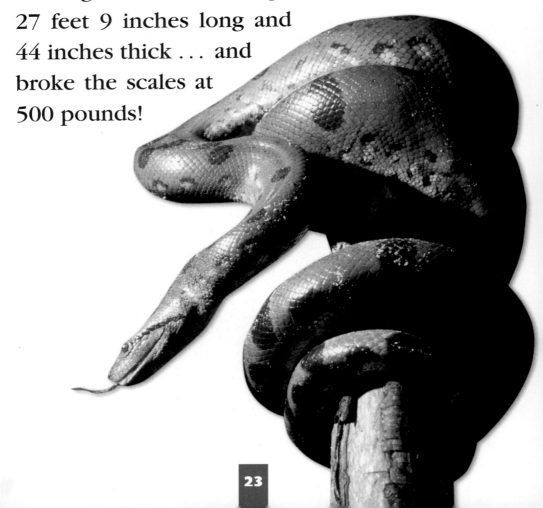

Rarest Snake

Despite its name, the Antiguan racer (*Alsophis antiguae*) is not the record-holder in speed (below). It is the **Rarest Snake** and lives on Great Bird Island off the coast of Antigua in the Lesser Antilles. A recent count found only 80 of these snakes alive. Black rats not native to the island had reversed the roles of hunter and prey — now rats were hunting snakes. Since the rats were removed, the snake population is growing. To save this species, scientists plan to bring in more colonies of racers to other islands.

Fastest Land Snake

Nobody wants to be caught by the black mamba (*Dendroaspis polylepis*)! The **Fastest Land Snake** lifts its head and slithers up to speeds of 10 to 12 miles per hour for short bursts across flat ground (left). The deadly snake lives in southeastern Africa and sometimes sneaks into people's homes. While its skin color is gray, the inside of its mouth is black. That's not something you want to see, because the mamba's venom is deadly. This snake is shy, but if scared, the first 3 feet of its body will spring up into the air before its fangs strike the target!

Smelly Snakes

People were afraid of a snake's forked tongue before they learned this is a snake's "nose" to the world. Smells help the snake find food or avoid danger. Most snakes don't have good eyesight, but their sense of smell is better than humans! The tongue catches scent particles. Its forked shape fits perfectly between two pockets inside the mouth (above).

Pit vipers, boas, anacondas, and pythons can track changes in temperature. They have extra organs in front of their eyes. These snakes *see* the heat coming from warm-blooded animals – it looks orange or red – and can follow the animal's movements (left).

Most Widely Distributed Venomous Snake

The **Most Widely Distributed Venomous Snake** slithers through several countries, from West Africa through the Middle East and into India (see map). The saw-scaled or carpet viper (*Echis carinatus*) likes to burrow under the sand. This hide-and-bite behavior makes the snake hard to spot before it strikes. Its raspy hiss sounds like a saw, but the noise is not enough warning. Small at 11.8 inches long, this snake has killed more people than any other species.

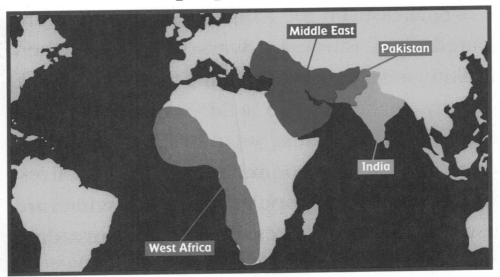

Snakes, even the dangerous ones, are more scared of us (above). Always be careful when walking near a snake's home and don't pick up any snakes in the wild. Some snakes are extremely dangerous, but they play important roles in the environment and in our lives. Snakes control the populations of rats, which are usually the animals responsible for spreading diseases among humans.

Snakes are also our only cure if they poison us. **Antivenin** is medicine created by doctors to treat a poisonous snake's bite (below). The medicine is the snake's poison changed by other chemicals. Scientists have learned that snake venom can possibly cure serious diseases, such as heart attacks and cancer. Some reptiles really are *saving* lives!

We can learn much by studying reptiles.
These animals have lived longer than people because
of their survival skills in an ever-changing world.

Guinness World Records will share more incredible reptile
discoveries with you from around the world!